Location Guide Book

"Take your memories back down the stretch of memory lane to those heady days of Herne the Hunter, magic and witchcraft, Wickham Village, Kings and soldiers, outlaws and heroes, and visit the very locations they used in the 1980's television show. Stand in the historical sets of castles, priories, woodlands and forests; follow in the footsteps of the cast."

Acknowledgements

We would like to thank all contributors to this guide, the fans, for helping to make this possible. Without your dedication to this great television show, some of these locations would still remain hidden. Keep the Robin of Sherwood fires burning!

Dedication

We would also like to dedicate this guide to all the fans of the show. Feedback we have received, from fans that have already purchased this guide and used it to visit some of the locations, have warmed our hearts; seeing their faces as they describe how they have stood amid the castle walls of the locations and seen what their heroes have seen has been a tremendous achievement.

Introduction

Having always harboured a fascination and passion for medieval architecture, and a lifelong appreciation of the iconic 1980's television show Robin of Sherwood©, the 'Trail of Robin of Sherwood' guide was born.

The production teams for the show worked amazing visual magic to bring each location to life, creating just the right blend of medieval atmosphere to enhance the Robin of Sherwood© experience, and it was this fascination that helped to inspire this guide book and our website. Memories of those wonderful locations - the 12th century Norman castles and abbeys, priories and forests - each were seemingly a character themselves in the program, all helping to add that air of mysticism that still haunts the viewer to this day.

Within the pages of this guide, we hope to bring you a comprehensive look at the locations as they are now to help you plan and go on your own location hunts. The feeling of following in the footsteps of the show, seeing the locations with your own eyes, is an exciting experience and only enhances watching the show all the more.

Happy location hunting!
The Trail of Robin of Sherwood team

Through the 'Handy Hints' boxes, this guide book will show you what to look for, where to look for it, how it was used, even which episode it was used in, to bring the world of Robin of Sherwood© closer to you.

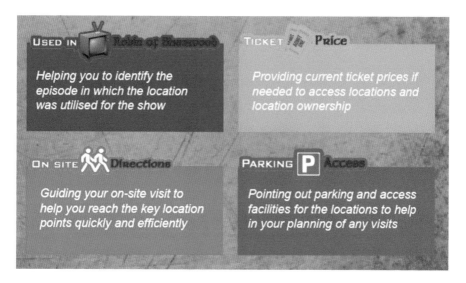

USED IN Robin of Sherwood
Helping you to identify the episode in which the location was utilised for the show

TICKET Price
Providing current ticket prices if needed to access locations and location ownership

ON SITE Directions
Guiding your on-site visit to help you reach the key location points quickly and efficiently

PARKING P Access
Pointing out parking and access facilities for the locations to help in your planning of any visits

Index

Places you can visit on your own Robin of Sherwood Road Trips covered in this Location Guide; some are free, some require ticket purchases, and some are privately owned and would need advance permission before attendance.

South East - Kent & East Sussex
Rochester Castle, Kent
Bodiam Castle, East Sussex

Northumberland
Alnwick Castle
Bamburgh Castle
Hulne Priory
Brinkburn Priory
Longhoughton Steel Beach

South Wales
Kidwelly Castle
Caldicot Castle
Chepstow Castle

Cornwall
St Michaels Mount
Rinsey Cliffs

Wiltshire
Tithe Barn, Bradford on Avon
Lacock Abbey
Malmesbury Abbey
Great Chalfield Manor
Bowood House Estate and Garden
Castle Combe (Manor House Golf Club)

Somerset
Blaise Castle Estate
Mells Park Estate
Chew Valley Lake
Round Wood, Lower Milton
Cleeve Abbey
Brent Knoll
Hinton Priory
Farleigh Hungerford Castle
Wells Cathedral
Wookey Hole Caves
Cheddar Gorge
Burrington Ham, Blagdon
Berrow Beach
Flax Bourton
Leigh Woods
High Littleton
Pro Cathedral

Gloucestershire
Berkeley Castle

Rochester Castle, Kent

Although Rochester Castle was not used as a filming location within the show, its connection with Robin of Sherwood is just as recognisable.

The appearance was as a backdrop on the Clannad album cover "Legend", the most excellent soundtrack for Robin of Sherwood. If you don't own a copy, make it your priority to get one … immediately!

TICKET Price

Rochester is under the administration of English Heritage and, gaining access to the location will require purchasing tickets which, if you're not a member, will cost (at time of print) £6.20 entry per adult.

PARKING P Access

The visiting fan needs to know that there is no parking directly on site at the castle, however there are a number of Pay & Display (coin operated) car parks located within a short walk from the entrance. There is a free of charge coach park located in nearby Corporation Street, and a coach drop off point at the rear of the visitor information centre.

Rochester Castle is a 12th Century keep, very fitting for the time period for the show, and the whole castle sits near the River Medway in Kent. The album cover itself contains a view of the side of Rochester Castle (along with a character shot of Michael Praed as Robin) and the familiar features of the crenelated tower can be seen in the background. Once on site, use the rounded tower as the focal point to identify the angle.

Bodiam Castle, East Sussex

Bodiam Castle only has one appearance in Robin of Sherwood which was a fleeting glance during the Series 3 opening episode "Herne's Son" as an exterior distance shot of Huntingdon Castle

Prices (at time of printing) are £7.80 per adult, and both yearly and daily opening times can be found on the National Trust website.

There is a main car park on site which is a short 400 yard walk to the castle entrance. There is also a main gift shop and tea room facility provided by the National Trust should the mood take you

The second of two South East locations for Robin of Sherwood, this 14th century castle was used in the episode for the exterior of Huntingdon Castle in numerous shots. One of the most memorable cut scenes from that episode is the arrival of Owen of Clun and his men by horseback.

Trying to locate the exact position of the camera shot is difficult with rural habitats that may not have been present during the filming stages but are very noticeable now. We surmise that the angle of the shot would have been far out into the fields beyond with little or minimal view of any existing local population residences within that field of view.

However, this is a very beautiful castle with a moat and bridge and is part of the National Trust network of historical properties. Access to the castle itself, which has a ruined interior and not actually used the show, is for the location hunter's personal choice but well worth a visit whilst you are there.

Alnwick Castle, Northumberland

USED IN Robin of Sherwood

Alnwick Castle was used exclusively in: Robin Hood and Sorcerer, The Prophecy & The Witch of Elsdon. It was also the main exterior castle shot for Nottingham Castle for much of the first 2 series

ON SITE Directions

If this is your current destination, walking down the main drive from the ticket office, you're greeted with the awesome sight of Alnwick Castle itself, spreading out to your right as you approach the main gatehouse. The grandeur of this stone construction is evident.

From a Robin of Sherwood point of view, it's easy to see why they started here for Robin Hood and the Sorcerer. The first location is through the main gatehouse and into the outer bailey field which was made famous in the show as the escape scene from the dungeon in the first episode. Walking around the outer walls, you could almost see Michael Praed racing across the battlements towards the door at the corner tower and Gisburne almost falling over a pig.

The section between the gatehouse and the inner courtyard was the next scene, memorable by Robert Addie on horseback in full battle armour, escorting Marion to Kirklees and receiving his instructions from the Sheriff and Abbott Hugo. This area was also used in 'The Prophecy' with the arrival of Prince John into the area.

The inner courtyard is your next location, remembering how the production crew had dressed the scene with soldiers and the alarm bell platform. Leave the inner courtyard, that was also used in The Witch of Elsdon for the brief moment that Robin rode in to rescue Jeanette's husband, and make your way around the castle to the outer bailey at the back for the wonderful scene of the Silver Arrow Competition.

The castle is privately owned but open to the general public and charges ticket prices and car parking prices separately. There is also a garden but for Robin of Sherwood location hunters you do not need to enter. Tickets purchased on the main website are cheaper than the gate price, currently (at time of printing) is £14.00 each online

From the car park, there is quite a walk to the entry point, as shown. Despite the distance, the castle does open out and ensure you have your camera ready for some great exterior photographic opportunities.

Within the castle, it is mainly even ground and an optional tour of the main buildings.

Bamburgh Castle, Northumberland

Bamburgh Castle appeared in the pilot episode of 'Robin Hood and Sorcerer' as the home of the evil Baron Simon de Belleme. It was later depicted as a ruin, within the story line of 'The Enchantment' highlighting a revolt against him following the pilot episode. However, the ruins in that episode were located at Chepstow Castle (South Wales).

ON SITE — Directions

Depending on your willingness for exercise (and the tide), you can view the castle from the beach, as shown in the episode, first before going into the castle itself to see the locations for both the battle and the escape.

The exterior of the outer bailey was used primarily for the battle scene at the end of the second part to Robin Hood and the Sorcerer with camera angles that took in the Norman Keep and the gate leading to the lighthouse.

For the second location on this site, you will need to go on the tour of the main castle. Once inside the main bed chamber, you descend some stairs to the right of the door you came in. At the bottom of the stairs you go left into a room with columns and steps at the other side of the room. The ceiling and columns are unmistakeable. This room was used as the guardroom at
Nottingham Castle during the escape of the prisoners, where Much fought the drunken guard. The large chains you see in the episode by the door they run out of are still there.

The keep doorway, which is not used now on the main tour, but which was used as the Merries exited to battle Gisburne and the soldiers, is accessible from the exterior as you walk the grounds.

 TICKET Price

The castle is privately owned but open to the general public and charges ticket prices. Robin of
Sherwood location hunters will need to purchase tickets for the main tour (prices currently
unknown) to see the Armoury.

PARKING P Access

The car park is on site and there is a small walk up the entry ramp to the main gate and the ticket office. Beach access is free and over rough, uneven terrain.

 **ON SITE Directions**

The lovely location of Hulne Priory, in Northumberland, is a very well-known location for all Robin Hood fans ... and not just Robin of Sherwood! Filming also took place here for the 'infamous' Kevin Costner version of "Prince of Thieves".

You can see why Robin of Sherwood production chose this area to film in, with Hulne Park being quite a vast open park land with great visual shots to bring a medieval world to life.

For visiting fans, it's a walk rather than a drive through Hulne Park if you want to see the Priory ruins and the infamous doorway into the RoS location. This is, however, home to a private house in the grounds of the priory but access is allowed into the main area.

It appears in the show twice, where Robin escorts Marion to Kirklees Abbey by horse, watched over by Nasir who is hidden from view. It then again makes another appearance as Tuck goes to warn Marion of the 'master plan' by Simon de Belleme.

Hulne Priory's exterior appeared in the first episode 'Robin Hood and Sorcerer'. If you think the word "Kirklees", you would probably know all about this place.

From Alnwick town, head out on Ratten Row from the B6346 and you can park along there toward the park entrance.
You now have quite a walk through the Hulne Park saw mill gate, following Farm Road to a right on Iron Bridge Drive, then a right before Palmstrother Drive to the Priory.

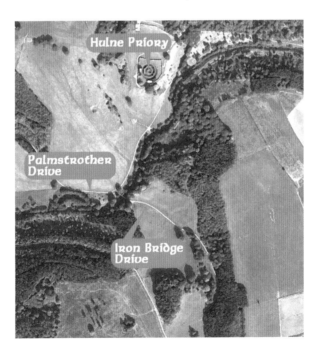

Brinkburn Priory, Northumberland

The Priory is approximately 4 1⁄2 miles south-east of Rothbury, off B6344, and is sign posted. The car park is free of charge and located around 400 meters from the site, with a short walk down through the trees to the ticket office, gift shop and the priory itself. If you're early enough there is a small layby approximately 100 metres from the reception, which will accommodate a maximum of five cars.

ON SITE Directions

Nestled in the woods at the bottom of long access walk lies Brinkburn Priory, a small but perfectly formed piece of 12 Century architecture. It was here that we discovered the cleverness of the filming crew and their ability to change a camera angle and make the same building look like a different place.

Walking inside the main building, the scene instantly grabs you. Close your eyes and you can visualise the Sheriff, Abbott Hugo and the Baron de Belleme discussing Marion's 'future'. The stain glass windows that acted as the backdrop for that scene are wonderful. We have two other scenes filmed on the inside here: Marion talking to the Baron, dressed in her nun outfit
and Robin's entrance into the Castle Belleme to face the Baron (going in) and Nasir (going out).

Cleverly, the camera angle removes the main 'hall' and takes in the side area looking down towards the main door with the columns on the left. Moving through the other door (the one that the Sheriff and the others came through during the episode), takes you out into the mini cloisters at the back.

You can see these in the episode after the Silver Arrow contest where they are walking with their cloaks blowing in the breeze and a monk walking around in the background.

Ticket Price

The priory itself is another belonging to the English Heritage network of properties and, as such, an entrance fee is a necessity to see the Robin of Sherwood locations. At time of printing, the fee is £3.90 per adult and the opening times can be found on the main English Heritage website.

Used in Robin of Sherwood

Brinkburn Priory was utilised twice by the filming crew in the pilot episode of Robin Hood and Sorcerer. Its distinctive windows and columns were noticeable as the room the Sheriff retired to after the Silver Arrow competition, appearing as part of the Belleme audience chamber and it was also the corridor for Castle Belleme interior where Robins bow was set alight by black magic and he fought Nasir.

The beach scene at Fairlight Cove was filmed here, with Much on horseback warning Robin of Marks traitorous intentions to murder Marion's father, Sir Richard of Leaford, before he could reach the King in 'The Prophecy'

This is a sand and rock beach near to the town of Amble. Access is by a single track road, running past some isolated holiday cottages, and parking can be found along the left road on the grass areas as you approach the beach.

Kidwelly Castle, South Wales

ON SITE Directions

The small town of Kidwelly in South Wales is home to a glorious Norman Castle. Despite it being a ruin, the construction, the design and the remains are still awe inspiring. Take a walk around the castle, known to Robin of Sherwood fans as Clun Castle from Series 3 episode of Herne's Son.

Faced with the initial view of the gatehouse, fans will remember 'Frederick the Peddler' coming around the corner with his donkey and banging on the portcullis. The area where Much stood with the donkey, ready to pull the poles out, is very evident down to the side with the backdrop of the houses in the distance coupled with the river that John and Tuck ran up from with the tree trunks to wedge the gate.

Heading through the main gates, takes you into the gatehouse, where, immediately to your left, is the room where they housed the portcullis gears, and where Will cut the rope. The main access through the gatehouse leads you into the outer bailey and the famous scene after Nasir was liberated and Marion rescued, the gang walked through with Owen of Clun as their hostage.

TICKET Price

Kidwelly Castle is owned by Cadw, the Welsh Historic Environment Services, and ticket prices for entry will cost £4.00 per adult (at time of printing). Opening times vary and it is recommended to check the Cadw website prior to visiting.

There is a car park on site, next to the ticket office.

After a short walk to the main entrance, the location is on even ground but does have difficult stairwells if you intend on going up to the battlements.

This castle will be familiar to fans as Clun Castle from the Series 3 episode of 'Herne's Son'. The band of Merries needed to break into the castle to rescue Marion and discover Nasir as Owen's champion.

Episodes of Swords of Wayland, The Inheritance, and Time of the Wolf were all filmed here.

Going to this location you will find yourselves in the town of Caldicot, heading down the winding track-way in the Country Park and viewing the frontage of this lovely castle used for many scenes in Robin of Sherwood.

The familiar view of the drawbridge and entrance will greet you first, used as Grimstone Abbey in The Time of the Wolf. To the left of the bridge is the grassy area used by the monks in the episode as they tended their vegetable garden, and subsequently, where the Sons of Fenris attacked!

The next memorable scene is from the end of the episode, the Merries lined up by the drawbridge in the dry moat, trying to entice the Sons of Fenris out. It can be a difficult step to get into the moat depending on the level of nettles (don't wear shorts!!!).

Leaving the episodes of Time of the Wolf, brings us to The Inheritance. In this episode, fans will recall Ray Winstone scaling the wall on Caerleon Castle, the very wall that is to the left of the gatehouse at Caldicot before you get to the round tower on the corner. The rest of the internals to Caerleon Castle were filmed mainly at Chepstow Castle.

The entrance was again used in The Swords of Wayland for Gwyddian Castle. It seems so simple to just drop a few flags over the windows in the episode and make it another location in the show. Both Marion and Tuck, Robin and Marion escaping on horseback, and Morgwyn riding out, all made the filming schedule here.

Even though the exterior shows you all there is to see from a Robin of Sherwood perspective, you can optionally head inside and have a walk around the grounds. It is still a fantastic castle, with many of the rooms in the towers intact. The canon, in the centre of the courtyard is of special historic interest, being from Lord Nelsons ship.

 Ticket Price

The castle is privately owned but accessible to the general public and admission is now free (except on event days, so check in advance). Check the castle website for daily and yearly opening times.

 Parking P Access

From M4 take junction 23a and B4245 to Caldicot. Caldicot Castle is sign posted from B4245.
Parking is free of charge at the castle with a large area for cars behind the tree line at the front of the castle entrance. The grounds surrounding it are extensive, used by the local dog walkers etc. and has uneven surfaces so watch your step if you decide to go for a stroll.

Chepstow Castle, South Wales

ON SITE Directions

Chepstow Castle sits on the border between England and Wales, the Severn River running closely alongside. For Robin of Sherwood, Chepstow hosted a number of classic scenes here, as well as some other minor ones.

The first scene you really get to is one in The Inheritance. From the ticket office / main shop, head up the steps to the Kitchen and you're standing in the corridor used during the episode when Much thought he heard the banquet.

Head down the stairs to your right and into the wine cellar. The wine cellar was used many times. To start with it was used as the old banqueting hall in Caerleon Castle. Next, look at the back wall of the cellar and picture Marion on a pentagram in the first ever episode. Lastly, turn around and look at the window for The Enchantment and Gisburne's jewellery theft through this window while trying to get at the Eye of Satan gargoyle.

Head back up the steps, through the outer bailey following the path, towards the inner bailey for the next scene. Stop before you enter the inner bailey and look about. This access gate was used in The Enchantment and was 'blocked' off, forcing the cast members through the little door to the left. It was the main access to the ruins of Castle Belleme. Step on through and you'll be faced with the Norman keep ahead of you.

The Baron, standing framed in the doorway up there, should help you frame the scene. Look to your left and you will see the ramparts that the cast had to fight their way along during the episode which is still accessible. You can head to the left and get up onto the top if the mood takes you.

Head past the keep on the path, through the inner bailey at the back and out to the Barbican. Welcome to the Caerleon Castle set. To go up to where Much and Isadora had their firing positions, go left at the end of the bridge (although there is another way up back in the inner bailey to the left) and up the spiral staircase. There is a doorway to your left that takes you back
towards the inner bailey, where Robin in the episode had his sword fight with one of the mercenaries. From the mid-landing keep going up and you'll get to the top where Much and Isadora stood.

The entrance into the barbican served as the main entrance into Caerleon and on most visiting days these gates are closed. It is a bit of stroll now back out of the castle and around the side.
For the episode of The Inheritance a nice access bridge was constructed to get up to the gates, signs of which have now long gone but with a little imagination you can picture it.

 **Price**

Chepstow Castle is owned by Cadw, the Welsh Historic Services, and ticket prices for entry will cost £4.50 per adult (at time of printing).

Opening times vary and it is recommended to check the Cadw website prior to visiting.

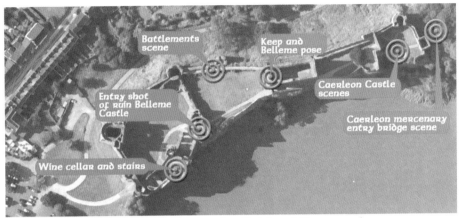

Fig – Chepstow Castle layout plan for Robin of Sherwood scenes

This is a very memorable view from the episode of Swords of Wayland, where St Michaels Mount was filmed as Ravenscar Abbey exterior.

Cornwall bound and it is to Marazion and St Michaels Mount. The Mount is beautifully lit at night and a wonder for all in the early morning light.

You will need to time your own visit with the sea and wait until the tide goes out to walk across the wonderful causeway to the Mount.

Once you get on the island, walk past the church graveyard, keeping it on your left and go up towards the back of the houses immediately in-front of you and you'll see the arch straight away.

The family crest is on the top of it now but that was probably obscured for the show with the Celtic cross.

Robin of Sherwood filming on the Mount was limited to the arch and a tour of the castle above is optional. If you decide to do the tour, there is a cost per ticket of £8.50 per adult (at time of printing). The walk up the side of the mount to the castle is very good for the thighs and the view is spectacular and well worth the trip up (although if you're there just for Robin of Sherwood, then you don't need to go up there if all you want to see is the arch).

Keep a close eye on the tide as it comes in quickly and cross the causeway, heading over the beach to the left were it is believed the angle to film Michael Praed when he looks towards 'Ravenscar' and the shot where Morgwyn is chased by the Hounds of Lucifer were recorded.

Photos courtesy of André Weber

Rinsey is a tiny village in Cornwall, west of Helston. There is a beautiful beach between the car park and the cliffs, though it is rather secluded and might never be crowded. On the small coastal path to the beach you can already see the cliffs in the background.

The locations that Robin of Sherwood production used for the various shots of Robin climbing back up the cliff face, the Merry Men taking a escorting a captured Robin to Morgwyn, and Herne's eventual appearance, are all still instantly recognisable today. Just like old architecture that still stands the test of time, the cliffs at Rinsey seem to be weathering the storms of nature very well.

The plateau on which all the cliff sequences were filmed is quite small the camera man merely had to turn around himself to shoot most of the scenes. In particular the specific rock on which Robin sat to relax after climbing up the cliffs is still untouched by time.

PARKING P Access

From Marazion, take the A394 along the coast road towards Rosudgeon and Breage.

After you pass Paa Sands Golf Club on your right, you will reach the village of Ashton. Rinsey lane is the second right turn in the village. Turn down Rinsey Lane and follow it all the way to the car park at the end of the road and coastal path.

From there you can access the coastal path direct to the filming location. As it is a coastal path, there may be areas of uneven ground and difficult terrain.

The Tithe Barn is located 1/2 mile south of town centre of Bradford-on-Avon off the B3109 and the car park has charges applied so you'll need some additional change to hand. It is only a short walk to the barn from there.

English Heritage own the Tithe Barn, however there is no ticket access and is free of charge to visit.

ON SITE Directions

It is difficult to begin to count the amount of times this wonderful structure was seen in Robin of Sherwood, but think 'main hall Nottingham Castle' (or any other castle scene in the show, for that matter) and then walk into this building. The opening times are generally 10:30am until 4pm most days but change over the Christmas seasonal periods. Check the main English Heritage website for those times.

The first thing that hits you here is the atmosphere. Not surprising this was the key location for Nottingham Castle. Looking around the barn, you get a real sense of history, especially the timber roof beams. It's only looking back at the show you realise how much the set builders actually had to do to convert this place into the main hall of Nottingham (and not forgetting
Huntingdon Castle hall in Herne's Son of course, and Gwyddian). You may have expected to be able to 'go upstairs', as the show leads you to believe, but that whole rear of the hall you see on the show was constructed.

Lacock Abbey, Wiltshire

PARKING P Access

Parking here can be a little tricky at times. There is a Pay & Display car park 200 yards away, or there is free parking if you can get on the roadside. From the ticket office, it is quite a walk to the Abbey.

TICKET Price

This is a National Trust property and you can, as part of your ticket purchase, go on the main tour of the upper abbey but there are no Robin of Sherwood scenes filmed up there. A ticket to the whole property will cost £12.90 each per adult (at time of printing). Check the National Trust website for daily and yearly opening times as this may vary.

ON SITE Directions

Walk past the main building steps, and heading round the right side of the building to your left, make your way to the real reason you came here: the Cloisters.

How many times was this place used? Several. In Cromm Cruac it was Tuck's home of Thornton Abbey where he had his altercation with the Abbott. The famous library in the episode was also filmed here. In The Pretender it was used for the Abbey of St Oswald of Angouleme, where Queen Isabella visited and was ambushed by Gisburne. Finally, it was seen briefly in Robin Hood and the Sorcerer for Kirklees Abbey.

The biggest scene was in The Pretender. After going through the door, walk around the cloister corridor to the first open room on your right (not up the little stairs … keep going). This was the main room in that episode where Arthur of Brittany fired upon the Queen and the fight broke out. Going back out of this, turn right, and walk down to the end of this section and through the doorway, bearing right. The room with the columns in housed the tied up monks and the small doorway to the back left of the room continues the story.

Go through the little door and you're in a small room with a triangular shaped column and window behind it. When this is lit up, you'd remember it as the scene where Arthur and Robin rolled around the walls fighting each other.

Just to the right of where you came in to this small room is yet another door. Go in there and there's the room where the Queen faces Arthur for the first time.

This is a fabulous location, mainly due to the fact that you can picture the flow of the episode and actually walk it from room to room. You should leave Lacock suitably impressed.

In Swords of Wayland, this location became the 'surface' entrance to Ravenscar Abbey with its distinctive archway and internal columns where the procession of the Nuns in the coven paraded through the Abbey with the Swords of Wayland held aloft.

There is a large Pay and Display to the north of the Abbey positioned off Gloucester Road and is only a short walk across the river and up a series of steps to the rear of the Abbey itself, and also many other car parks and shopping streets littered around the town.

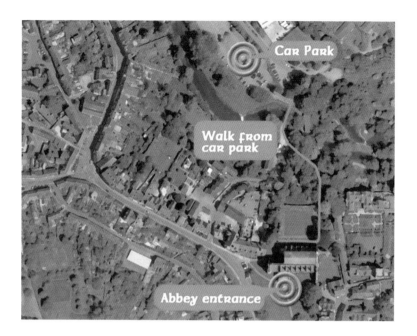

On the image: Car Park, Walk from car park, Abbey entrance

The Abbey at Malmesbury sits high over the town. Although it was only used in one episode, it heralds the most ornate doorway you will ever see on your tour. For the location hunter, the Abbey is free to enter (however, a kindly donation goes towards the upkeep) and the only charges you will incur for this location are for the car park. The doorway, as keen fans will recognise was used in 'The Swords of Wayland' as the main entrance for Ravenscar Abbey. Watching the show back again, you'll see it a couple of times: when Morgwyn of Ravenscar escorts the Sheriff to his horse and Verdilais greeting the coven members into the Abbey for the 'coming of Lucifer', not forgetting Robin stealing in at the end to save the day.

Go on inside for the next scene in the show and you'll recall the sword carrying ceremony. The ornate facade at the rear of the Abbey was constructed for the show and is not there now, taking it back to how it would have looked in the 12th Century. The ceiling is really breath-taking, so don't forget to look up! There is a little room at the top to the right where, legend has it, sick nuns could attend mass without infecting others. That was also used in the show when a couple of 'evil nun' followers sat up there. The exterior to Ravenscar Abbey was filmed at St Michaels Mount in Marazion (Cornwall) and the interior (except the crypt) was filmed here, so you can appreciate the travelling about the actors had to do when filming. This is a beautiful Abbey and is well worth a visit.

ON SITE Directions

From a physical location, Great Chalfield Manor is quite close to Bradford-on-Avon and therefore would be a good one to schedule a visit to in addition to the Tithe Barn.

As mentioned, Robin of Sherwood dressed it for Leaford Grange in 'The Power of Albion' episode. The area at the front of the main gates where the cart was set up for the Sheriffs spy is still nicely trimmed. Much came from the side road, running in disguised as a wood collector, sneaking past Richard of Leaford (George Baker) and 'forcing' his way in to see Marion when Robin was shot in the leg.

It was assumed that the chapel on the grounds was utilised in the Cross of St Ciricus. However, the small chapel was certainly not used in the show, despite location lists on the Internet mentioning as such.

The Power of Albion was the episode in which this location first appeared. The archway entrance into the main courtyard was the point of entry for Much attempting to reach Marion at her home of Leaford Grange

This location is one of the National Trust property network and will cost £8.70 per ticket (at time of printing). There are tours of the main manor house and access to the gardens, but Robin of Sherwood used this location as a primarily exterior angle so it is up to you if you want to go on the tour.

The location itself is situated off B3107 via Broughton Gifford Common. Follow the sign for Broughton Gifford (be warned it is a

narrow lane).The parking is free of charge here and on the grass verge on the exterior of the property.

Bowood House and Gardens, Wiltshire

Car park & ticket office

Waterfall location

The location, like Alnwick, is privately owned but accessible to the general public. There is a ticket price for the House and Gardens of £11.00 (at time of printing) but Robin of Sherwood was only filmed in the garden at the cascade.

There is no car parking charge but this location has quite a long walk through the estate to the cascade (see plan). Visiting fans may want to make a day of this location as the house and gardens are quite extensive in beautiful parkland.

The Robin of Sherwood crew came here for one location only; the fabulous cascade and the subsequent Robin versus Little John quarterstaff battle.

You can hear the cascade long before you can see it. Take a walk through the grounds, from the ticket shop and make your way left of the lake on the path. It winds its way down a slope and then you'll hear it. There's an access path the takes you down to the cascade itself, and you'll recognise the scene. The cascade isn't running as much water as it used to do, being on a controlled gate, but it is still instantly recognisable from the show. Obviously the little bridge Robin and Little John fought upon was put in for the show but you can still get to both sides of the cascade for any necessary 're-enactments' if you're that way inclined.

The only location for Robin of Sherwood here was the waterfall fight between Robin and Little John in the pilot episode of Robin Hood and the Sorcerer, and the additional scene where Will knocks Robin into the water with Dicken and Tom by his side.

Certainly one of the biggest changes to a Robin of Sherwood location was this one. The Manor House Golf Club, as it now is, used to be the home of Wickham Village but now, all that remains, is the bridge over the old river.

For the visiting Robin of Sherwood fan, there are two accessible points to see the bridge; either from the golf club itself (if you don't mind a little walk observing the golf etiquette), or from the village. Both have a walk involved.

If your choice of access is from the golf course car park, head past the tenth hole down the hill at eleven, you will then see the bridge. If it is the village, you can park in the village and walk through the Manor House hotel grounds along the path directly to the bridge. In either case, watch your head and look out for golfers teeing off from the hill.

Filming the bridge in numerous episodes, none more so than The Betrayal for Robin and Roger De Carnac's final showdown, the area just off the bridge was the scene for Wickham village before it was converted to a golf course. Clearly, a great deal has changed over the years, namely the construction of a championship golf course (designed by the well known Peter Allis, no less) and players of this magnificent course have to play over the bridge from one fairway to another to reach the green beyond where Wickham used to be.

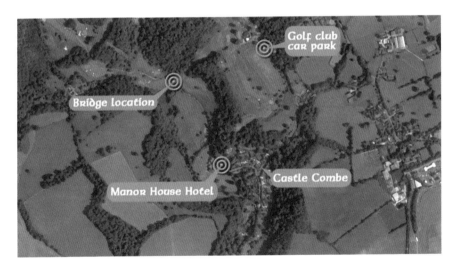

Both the bridge and the area to the side of the bridge appeared many times throughout Robin of Sherwood. Wickham was based here for a while, and the bridge was seen in The Betrayal with the final showdown battle, Rutterkin as the band of Merries were ambushed and leaped off the bridge, and The Pretender as Queen Isabella of Angoulême arrived on horseback.

Scenes in Robin Hood and the Sorcerer and Children of Israel. The woodland scenes here are fantastic and appeared in other episodes or scenes but which are now difficult to identify

 **ON SITE Directions**

Blaise Castle Estate is a large area, valuable to many locals as a good afternoon out while socialising and walking with friends and family, so it can get busy depending on what day or time you go. It is free to visit and walk around the estate.

Before setting foot on the grounds, it is advisable to scan an aerial view of the site as it is very large at 650 acres. You can reach the first location, on the hill by the castle, by heading directly across the field in front of the car park. Find the appropriate pathway that leads upwards (or if you're adventurous, track up the hill directly).

This first location was used in the final scene of the pilot Robin Hood and the Sorcerer. Fans will remember the cliff top speech that Robin gave to the others to persuade them that the loss of the lives of Dicken and Tom was worth the fight for freedom.

The backdrop to this scene looks out over the valley and the pathways below. You should recognise it as there is now a railing erected for safety. Heading back to the castle, you can hunt for your next location; that of the long stretch of 'grass road' they used to film the scene of the Sheriff returning to Nottingham with the cart in The Children of Israel. This area stretches for a long while, back towards the estates beyond the trees and, you can optionally walk the length of it. Various other woodland scenes were also filmed here, and with the acreage of the location, finding the specific ones since the show finished filming will be difficult.

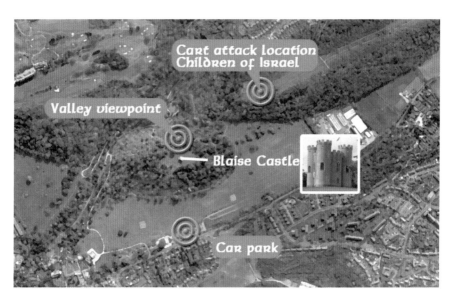

PARKING **P** ~~Access~~

Mells Estate is a large house & park, formerly part of the Glastonbury Abbey estate, and under private ownership. There sadly is no public access at all to any part of the grounds. Given that a large part of the estate woodlands is hired out for organised game shooting, it is not wise to trespass. Permission is required to access the grounds, and it is advisable to attempt this in writing prior to visiting.

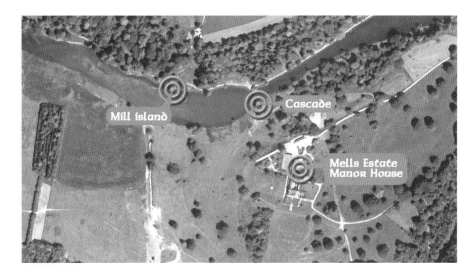

For the first series, Mells Park Estate near Frome, Somerset was largely used alongside Blaise Castle Estate and Leigh Woods in Bristol. Upon parking up and making your presence known at the main house, and following a short walk through the stable yard & gardens, you reach a huge pasture. To the right stretches Mells River, with sloping woodland on the opposite bank.

The first landmark that you see is the cascading weir, from the first episode where Muchs parents' Mill was located. The narrow stepping stone walkway across the waterfall to the opposite bank is barred and gated. This means that you are unable to explore the small island upon where they built the mill, with working water wheel. The waterfall was again used in "The Cross of Saint Ciricus" acting as the River Trent, where Gisburne borrows a raft to escape from Croxden after stealing the cross. Beyond the mill island it is now suspected that the flaming arrow ceremonies took place where the "river" squares toward the end of the water run; the filming environment looks a match.

Turning around from this point, you are at the foot of an old tree with wide and heavy overhanging branches. This was where the outlaws climbed up into to observe the Templars in "The Seven Poor Knights from Acre." Behind this, you can clearly see the escarpment where Loxley and Much ran towards, pursued by the Templars in one of the final scenes.

Following the line of the river upwards you come to the area where Loxley village was built. There is no sign of the jetty where the Normans knights disembarked but you can see the small inlet where it probably would have been, as well as the small island where they punted across from.

The scene of the notorious and ill-fated mud fight was filmed here, when part of the river was especially dry and had turned to mud. However, the passing of time makes identifying this area difficult. Presumably a part of the same river was used to place a log bridge over in Alan a Dale, where a mischievous Tuck takes on all challengers with his trusty staff!

A new location added to this wonderful location is very iconic; the flaming arrow scenes. It was once believed these ceremonies were filmed at Chew Valley Lake, but looking at the topography, the filming landmarks and also speaking with the cast at the 2016 Convention, it was confirmed the location for this was at the end of the river, heading left away from the main house.

Photos courtesy of Dan Rendell / Janet Reedman

For a more detailed look and walk around this large location, there is a car park at the top tip of the lake off Wally Lane that has picnic benches and other facilities.

This large lake is great for a nice walk, take a picnic and see all it has to offer. The location on offer here is the Nasir / Sarak duel area.

The only place does not have signs of civilisation in the background AND had access away from any main road was the route down to the sailing club to the waters edge. If the filming crew had been given permission to go down here, there's certainly a strong possibility it was down here as the reeds were a bit of a giveaway.

Once seen, carry onward, clockwise around the lake and head for the island. It was long believed that the arrow ceremony could have been filmed here and logic dictated to head for the island and the nearest land to it. However, since reviewing the footage, and the topographical area, it is now considered that the flaming arrow ceremonies for the first two series were filmed at Mells Park Estate.

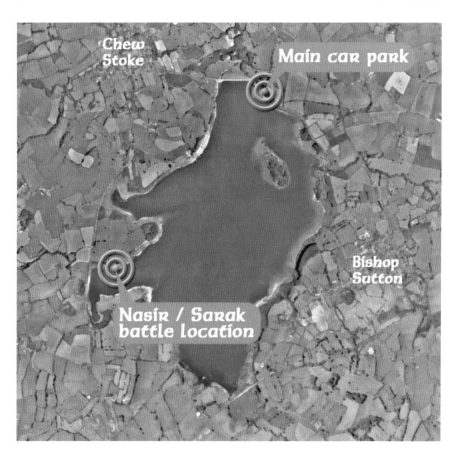

Round Wood at Lower Milton, near to Wookey Hole Caves, was the location for the fight in the finale of the 'Cross of St Ciricus' episode, Robert and Gisburne battling hand to hand, without realising that they are related.

Walk south, away from the main village on the Wells Road, passing the disused post office on your right and Chapel Antiques on your left. After a few hundred yards of walking past fields on either side you reach some more houses and a road on your left called Lime Kiln Lane.

Go up the lane and keep going past several large stone blocks placed in the road to prevent vehicles proceeding. The lane gets more narrow and disused looking and then there is a left hand turning which you should take.

The Lime Kilns are now visible to the right but keep going past more blocks and an old metal gate and you find yourself in the old quarry. On your left is a wall of reddish rock where the outlaws stood to view the fight on the cliff top to your front.

If you carry on through the narrow cutting in the rock and then double back to your right it is possible to follow a gentle ascent up the back of the cliff face and stand on the very spot where Robin and Gisburne fought it out. Be very careful here, the undergrowth is thick and tangled now. A stumble here could mean falling off the cliff.

Photos courtesy of Mike McGuinness

To reach the abandoned quarry, it's best to park in Wookey Hole Village, on the road outside the Inn or Church, however, it is quite a long walk from this point. Be warned, Wookey Hole village can get very busy in the holiday season with traffic visiting the caves there.

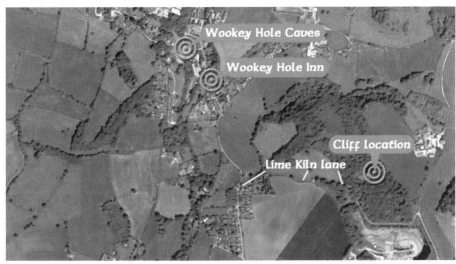

USED IN Robin of Sherwood

During the episode of Cromm Cruac, Tuck and Marion visited Thornton Abbey, first seeing it across the field. That view was here, at Cleeve Abbey. Several internal cut scene shots in the episode were also here.

The exterior to Thornton Abbey, Tuck's first monastic placement, was briefly seen in the episode of Cromm Cruac while he and Marion sought information from the Abbott. In actuality, it was the exterior of Cleeve Abbey in Somerset.

An English Heritage property, this was originally a Cistercian Abbey. Robin of Sherwood production only used this location for intermediate fill shots, with one exterior and one brief interior before the filming switched to Lacock Abbey.

You will find the shot used in the filming was taken in the surrounding field.

TICKET Price

For visiting fans there's an admission charge of £4.70 and a few minutes' walk from the car park to the entrance. Be sure to check the English Heritage website for daily and yearly opening times.

Brent Knoll, Somerset

 **ON SITE** **Directions**

Brent Knoll was a perfect location for the various, mysterious stone circles they used within the show.

This is, however, one of those locations without a specific parking allocation. For your own visit, it is recommended to head toward the church in Brent Knoll village at the base of the hill.
Park up in that vicinity because there is a path that leads from behind the church to the summit which has some shallow wooden steps toward the top.

Eventually, after a long walk up with the last 100 metres zapping whatever strength you have left, you will reach got to the top. Admire the view as you regain what breath you can.

 **USED IN** **Robin of Sherwood**

A little stroll around the top and you'll see which areas they used for Rhiannons Wheel in The Kings Fool and the Ring of the Nine Maidens in Time of the Wolf.

The list of episodes that were filmed at Hinton Priory is seemingly endless; The Swords of Wayland, Seven Poor Knights from Acre, Herne's Son, The Pretender, The Cross of St Ciricus, Adam Bell, The Betrayal, The Sheriff of Nottingham, and Rutterkin

Hinton Priory is privately owned, so you will need prior permission to visit this location. The owners are amicable and appreciate the Robin of Sherwood location for fans, so do not hesitate to contact them first.

The first building that hits you on arrival is the Chapter House; used frequently for many different scenes during the making of Robin of Sherwood. Start there first, heading inside and in the very first room you will find the first location: the Sheriff's bedroom in Seven Poor Knights from Acre and the 'meeting room' used in The Pretender where Sir Guy first met the usurper 'Arthur of Brittany'. Sticking with 'Seven Poor Knights' the entrance doorway is instantly recognisable from the episode. Move on through and you're walking down the same stretch of small corridor that they used for the dungeon access in The Swords of Wayland.

Go up the spiral stairs and you reach the first landing. Walking to the end of the small corridor and up a strangely familiar set of steps, you get to a large room which you will recognise as Marions bedchamber at Gwyddian Castle in The Swords of Wayland. Turning around to go out again and you realise that the room was used again, in 'Seven Poor Knights' for the guard room and dungeon where they kept Siward.

Back outside to the main courtyard, the wonderful ornate archway guides you through where you have that memorable scene in Herne's Son on the bustling market place and the Merries riding in on horseback. The first thing to see is the 'Amos Scafflock ale house' or the monk dining room as it used to be. This room, not only used in for the interior of the ale house, was also used from many different angles in Seven Poor Knights when the Merries had to break
into Leaford Grange. The window they slid through is around to the right and
the doorways they came in and out of are still looking good.

Moving around the building to the other side, you realise that this was the main Leaford Grange courtyard for Seven Poor Knights. From the courtyard of Nottingham Castle in The Sheriff of Nottingham to where King John sat in Rutterkin as he interrogated the prisoners before, the exterior for Warren Abbey used in The Pretender and the kidnap scene in Nottingham for Adam Bell, you get a real sense of the time they spent here.

ON SITE Directions

A magnificent castle perched on the side of a hill overlooking the valley, Farleigh Hungerford played host to several Robin of Sherwood episodes. Before you even get out of your car, you've driven through the first location: the main gatehouse. This was location for the scene in Alan-a-Dale with Marion and Much, in a cart with the others concealed in the back for the Sheriffs wedding.

Next you head over to the chapel entrance. This was the scene they used for Halstead Priory in The Time of the Wolf and Jason Connery came knocking on that very door. When visiting, this door is locked but for fans, there's another way around. Following the path around to the left (when facing the external chapel door) it leads around to the right alongside the chapel wall, we reached the next location: the main street for Nottingham Castle.

This small stretch of courtyard was dressed numerous times with people bustling here and there, market stalls set up either side or Norman guards on patrol. You'll remember it from episodes such as Seven Poor Knights with Siward on the run, Children of Israel where the riots against the Jews took place and from The Kings Fool when Gisburne 'ambushed' the Merries on their way to the castle to meet the King.

Step through into the very room off the main street they used for the De Talmont household. Standing back, you can let your imagination fill in the blanks. Not only was it used for the Children of Israel but it was also the potter's house in Seven Poor Knights when Robin, Marion and Will met up with him to discuss Siward. It was also used at the end of The Time of the Wolf where Robin came looking for Marion at Halstead for a brief shot.

Carry on around and past the steps at the end of the 'main street'. The other side of the chapel door comes around quickly. Go into the chapel. Apart from being a well maintained place, this was used as one of the final scenes in Robin of Sherwood with Marion revealing she was leaving the group in The Time of the Wolf. Cleverly, the production crew for the show built a false wall the other side of the signature font to give it that "12c Century" feel but the distinct wall recesses are still evident.

Head back out of the chapel and walk around to the right in the direction of the crypt entrance. This is the place where they shot the De Talmont donkey and the family leaving in that episode.

Ticket Price

This is an English Heritage location and access tickets cost (at time of printing) £4.30 per adult. It is also well worth going on the official voice recorded tour to learn about the castle. It is usually open from 10am until 6pm but it is wise to check yearly and daily times on their official website.

Episodes range from: Alan-a-Dale, Children of Israel, Seven Poor Knights from Acre, Time of the Wolf, and The Kings Fool

The main areas in Wells Cathedral, used during filming, were the Chapter House room, the stairs up to the Chapter House, and the upper staircase, for Robin Hood and the Sorcerer and The Swords of Wayland

Obviously owned by the Church, there is no direct entry fee but a donation to the upkeep is well worth the cost of the visit. If you want to take your camera, you'll need to buy a photo license from the small desk (at the time of printing this is only £3.50 or so but well worth it for the Robin of Sherwood location hunter).

Wells Cathedral does not have a direct car park but there are Pay & Display car parks around the town. You will need to follow the signs to find a suitable one of your own choosing.
For physical nearby locality, there is a car park a few streets away on Queen Street to the south east of the Cathedral.

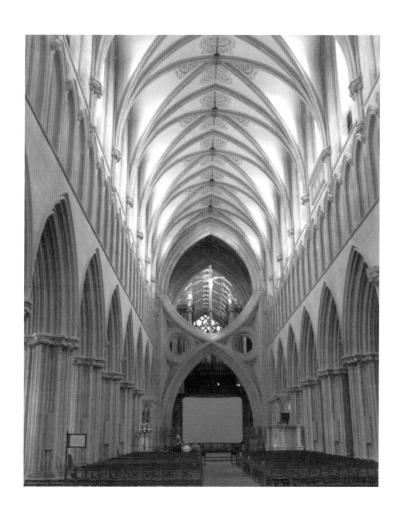

Take a walk around to the left and down past the cathedral organ, you'll see the door to the Chapter House steps on your left as you pass the clock. Step through and you'll be faced with the infamous steps in Nottingham Castle for Robin Hood and the Sorcerer.

Walk in the footsteps of Michael Praed in the first episode and ascend the stairs to the Chapter House on the right (where Marion's bedroom door was in the pilot episode). You'll recognise this room from The Swords of Wayland as the room where Morgwyn of Ravenscar interrogated Adam the Miller. As always said, don't forget to look up! The ceiling here is wonderful.

The stairs further upward were also seen in The Swords of Wayland as the members of
the coven arrived in turn, and Robin, having escaped capture, advanced downward to save the others dressed as a Hound of Lucifer and recover Albion from Morgwyn's grasp.

Such a wonderful location that has barely changed since the show was filmed.

All the scenes for Herne's cave interior needed a physical location, and this is it. Have a camera with a good flash to hand!

 **Price**

For this location, it is better to purchase your tickets online. This lowers the purchase price to £15.30 (at time of printing) from £18 each adult ticket.

If you have mobility issues, it might be best not to take this location on; there are steep steps
and slopes outside as well as within the caves, together with slippery surfaces. Be very careful.
Parking is on site a short walk from the ticket office, followed by the steep hike up to the cave entrance, and the long trek into the many caves.

You'll have to take the tour for this one.

It's really difficult to actually take photo's when on the tour so make sure you've got a camera with a good flash on it because the ambient lights tend to fade in and out randomly until it is time to move on from that area. Once you've had the introductory speech from the tour guide, you're taken down some steep steps and into the Witch's Kitchen that legend has it a witch lived in for many years, feared by the locals. This 'room' was used extensively in Robin of Sherwood for the interior to Herne's cave. The place where you stand on the tour is above where Herne had his table set up in the show. Be prepared prior to arrival in this area in order to take some quick fire flash images. The tour does not stay long and you'll only have as long as the tour guide's speech and the other visitors walking out afterward in order to take what images you need.

The rest of the tour is fascinating and well worth the trip. There are some great chambers down there that really blow you away, namely the Cathedral Chamber, which is as high as it is deep. This location is very near to **Round Wood** and would be a useful site to visit as well when planning your road trip.

 **USED IN** Robin of Sherwood

This location, and the gorge beyond was used in Robin Hood and the Sorcerer, Herne's Son - Part 2 and The Swords of Wayland

 **PARKING** Access

If you are approaching from the Chew Valley Lake side, towards Cheddar itself on the B3135, the Black Rock car park is on the left hand side of the road.

The walk to the first location is on uneven track, and the gorge beyond has varied terrain.

It's walking time again around the beautiful Cheddar Gorge in Somerset. The small car park at Black Rock is easy to miss as you round corners so be aware for the signpost.

Park, cross over, and start your walk up the incline, through the gate and along the nobbled pathway. After a short walk of about 5-10 minutes, you'll round a corner, the trees will vanish and you're staring at the distinctive Uffcombe Village rock face from The Swords of Wayland.

If you're feeling energetic you can scale the hill on the opposite side to capture the shot from the show. Going up the actual slope, where Much sat guard, is a little treacherous underfoot now due to several landslides leaving a pile of rubble at the foot of the slope. Carry on along the path you came in on with the Uffcombe slope on your left. It bends around to the right and the access to the field for the Uffcombe photo is on your right.

Keep going because you're heading for Hathersage now from the episode of Herne's Son - Part 2. Check our website map here for directions. A little way around, there's a gate with a turnstile next to it.

Go through it and almost immediately on your left is a small path going up. Keep going and it opens out into a field so head for the brow. Welcome to Hathersage! The headland where Little John and Much look to see Robin and Tuck on horseback is in sight.

The slopes and rocky outcroppings that served as the location for the final showdown between Robin and the Sheriff in The Greatest Enemy is the target for this site visit - Burrington Ham, Blagdon.

Take the B3134 from the A368 from Blagdon, drive up the road past the Burrington Inn on your left. Follow the road through the gorge for about half a mile and then park in the large layby on your left at the top of the gorge. There is a wooden signpost marked Burrington Ham so keep a ready eye for it.

The location has a free car park, though not too large, and from there it is a walk to the site itself over varied terrain. Take the left hand path from the car park and follow the path until it open out onto heathland, where you can walk on and come to 3 paths.

The outcropping filming that took place can be reached by taking the left hand or centre path. The centre path affords a more dramatic first view of the rocks so have your camera ready.

From the top of the rocks the view affords you an easy vista to place the approach of the Sherriff's men towards the trapped outlaws, although the trees and shrubs have altered dramatically since the show originally aired.

Photos courtesy of Mike McGuinness

PARKING P Access

You can, at the public access location, drive on to the beach itself, but this is not recommended. The sand and the subsequent gorse dunes at the rear are uneven and difficult terrain if you have mobility issues.

ON SITE Directions

It's a drive to the coast for this location. Berrow Beach was used as a substitute for the Holy Land, so get your toes out and head for the sand. There is no real specific place to travel to or park to access the beach, having several locations to do so, but there is a public area to park along the front. Drive along the main road through Berrow and you will find it signposted.

Once you're on the beach, you can see why it was used as a desert location, especially when the tide is out. When we arrived the sea was a heck of walk!

Still, there was very little to look for as the Nasir flashback scene in The Sheriff of Nottingham could have literally been anywhere along this stretch of sand. We know, during the Robin of Sherwood Convention in 2008, Mark Ryan had told us that they couldn't turn the camera angle aroundbbecause there were houses near enough directly in shot so that gives you an idea where they were for this location. He told us several funny stories about the camel, wanting to be in the camera shot and other things.

This location was used specifically for the Nasir "flashback" scenes in The Sheriff of Nottingham

This location only made one appearance in Robin of Sherwood. It played host to the episode of The Prophecy with the prisoners quarrying stones for the repair of the castle walls for Prince John's visit.

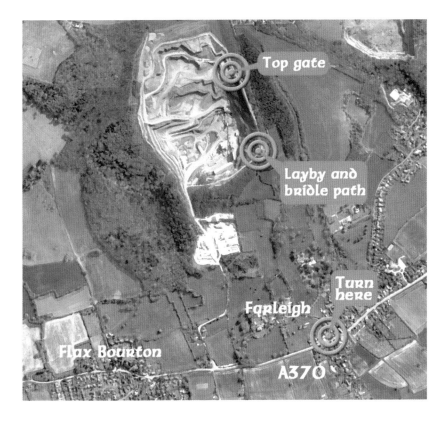

PARKING P **Access**

There is a layby at a stage of the bridle path alongside the quarry where you can park and walk up to the gateway at the top. However, as there are CCTV cameras positioned around the perimeter of the quarry, it is not advisable to see this location directly.

ON SITE **Directions**

On arrival in Flax Bourton, looking for the quarry, you will most definitely find it off the A370 that runs through the village. As it is owned exclusively by TARMAC, and activity there is always busy, you will be unable to walk on with your camera. Obviously the main crew for the shoot headed into the quarry itself through the main gates, but Michael Praed and the others
headed around the side to get to the top off Backwell Hill Road. There is an equestrian bridle path running alongside the quarry with nice warning signs ("If you hear a siren, dismount! Dynamite in use" or something similar.)

You may not want to trespass directly on TARMAC land unless you can gain prior private authorisation to enter with your hard hat and high-visibility jacket, and so the next best thing is the bridle path.

USED IN Robin of Sherwood

This location was used in various Sherwood Forest scenes for the show, and the lake there was used as Hernes cave exterior in The Enchantment

ON SITE Directions

Off the A369 through Abbots Leigh, take a walk through the greenwood and get back to nature for Leigh Woods.

Herne's Cave & Lake (Abbots Pool long & lat; 51.456265, -2.669016) is in a quiet area occupying a corner of the vast Leigh Woods in Bristol. Access to the lake is via a minor road off the main road, through residences, and the entrance comes up fast around a blind corner. Parked up in the parking bay there is a 3 minutes' walk to the pool.

Minutes down the clearly pointed out woodland path you come to the start of the lake. First it is advisable to head towards the grotto which is located on the opposite end of the lake, although it is not immediately visible at first due to overgrowth of the surrounding trees and bushes.

The lake itself takes about 10 minutes to walk around completely. It is still very recognisable from the episode, The Enchantment, where Robin steals the silver arrow from Herne's Cave. Immediately apparent is that the area in which Herne stood out on the jetty to welcome Marion, which is now overgrown. The cave is a modern addition and is purely an ornamental feature. Looking inside it's no more than about 10ft square however, in the episode you see Michael duck to go inside, but the interior for the filming is at another location.

Leaving the grotto, start to look for the area where Marion set out on the boat across the lake. You will not have to look far, in fact you may have already passed it. It is just a 100 feet away from the grotto, on the opposing corner. The proximity is cleverly concealed on the show by the use of dry fog.

The clump of trees near the water's edge is where the band of Merries stood remains and is still clearly identifiable as you will see.

Photos courtesy of Dan Rendell / Janet Reedman

The car park is a free of charge parking facility, with walking guides on boards around the area.
The overall terrain is uneven in places and is typical woodland surfaces.

When remembering the episode of Cromm Cruac, you may think about the pool where Gulnar cast his magic, and where the final slow motion battle took place. This is that location.

Cam Waterfall, sometimes known as Hallatrow Falls, or the Fairy Glen, is located in the village of High Littleton, North Somerset. It is located at the far end of Greyfield Woods, run by the Woodland Trust. The main entrance is about a mile off of the High Street (A39).

A hidden gem of a location, not on many lists out there, is High Littleton. Being close to Chew Valley Lake, Mells and Farleigh Hungerford Castle, it can be a combination of visits on your planned road trip.

From the High Street, drive down Greyfield Road and turn left to go to Greyfield Farm. You will find a small parking area for the woods near it. The area is a very popular walker's spot, so the car park tends to fill up very easily. It might be better to park in the nearest available space down the street and walk up, being careful not to block anyone's house entrance. Also worth noting is the road to the farm is quite bumpy and pot holed.

Once you enter through the woodland entrance, a sign greets you welcoming you to the woods. The falls are not marked on the map, but you will find it very easily. It will take you about 15 minutes to walk. You need to walk down the sloping woodland track for about 1 mile until you reach an open, long meadow. Crossing the meadow to the left corner will take you into a smaller woodland, called Stephens Wood.

Almost immediately upon entering you will see the River Cam ahead of you, with a footbridge crossing. Cross here and turning immediately left takes you around and up the side of a small gorge where the waterfall is situated. Progress slowly up to the top of the falls, and the area of the trees to the right is where the pathway down was marked with burning torches in the episode, and scene of the "slow motion" sword fight between the outlaws and Gulnar's dark disciples.

Photos courtesy of Dan Rendell / Janet Reedman

Various castle interiors were filmed here, along with the interior of Grimstone Abbey in Time of the Wolf and Caerleon Castle main hall in The Inheritance

The parking at this location is on the roadside with Pay & Display meters outside the cathedral which are quite constraining, with high rates charged for a short period of time.

A little piece of history amongst the concrete jungle, the Pro Cathedral was the Roman Catholic cathedral in Bristol until 1973. However, since being abandoned, it has now been converted into student accommodation for the University.

As a location hunter for Robin of Sherwood, this location is included in this guide purely as a historical site from the show. You can still visit this location and but the exterior shown here is now no longer the same as the pictures. Even though the interior was the only area to be filmed, you will be unable to go inside and see it for how it was portrayed in the show.

Berkeley Castle, Gloucestershire

This medieval castle location appeared in Series 3 as Nottingham Castle, most notably in the episode of 'The Betrayal' seeing the arrival of King John and Roger de Carnac.

Berkeley Castle is privately owned, and like Alnwick in Northumberland, charges an admission fee of £10 per adult, and £5.50 for children (at time of printing).

There is a family ticket available (2 adults and 2 children) and under 3 year olds go free.

There is a free car park adjacent to the castle entrance with a picnic area for visitors just wanting to take in the lovely view.

For Location Hunters with more of a mobility issue, it has many steps around the keep
and is not wheelchair accessible

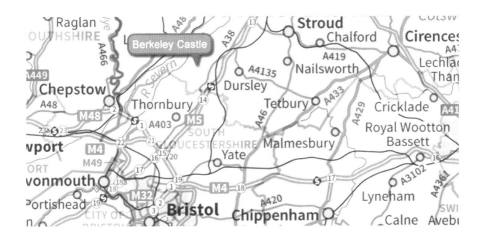

Robin of Sherwood Location Hunters will recognise this lovely castle in all its glory. By the third series, a move from Alnwick to Berkeley was made and it can be seen, dressed for King John's arrival, in 'The Betrayal'.

Although the castle itself has a tour of the inside of the keep, armoury, gallery and other lovely rooms, only the courtyard was used for filming of the show. Interior shots that followed were of the Tithe barn in Bradford on Avon. However, when visiting on a day trip, taking the tour will only be all the more enjoyable.

On the inside of the courtyard, the main camera shots used were pointing back toward the main entrance, the entry with the steps (as seen in the left picture on the opposite page) and a smaller entry with staircase following the wall around from the stepped doorway to the right of that image.

Just another fabulous location used in the show.

Thank you for purchasing our Location Guide. Happy Robin of
Sherwood Location Hunting to all the fans!

Printed in Great Britain
by Amazon